THE C.A.R.E. PACKAGE FOR RACIAL HEALING

Cultivating Awareness & Resilience through Empowerment

Isha W. Metzger, PhD

THE C.A.R.E. PACKAGE FOR RACIAL HEALING

Cultivating Awareness & Resilience through Empowerment

The C.A.R.E. Package for Racial Healing

Copyright ©2021 Isha W. Metzger
All rights reserved. Neither this book nor any parts within it may be sold or reproduced in any format without permission.

Printed in the USA
First Printing 2021

Published by Strive Publishing
3801 27th Avenue North Robbinsdale, MN 55422
www.strivepublishing.com

ISBN: 978-1-948529-16-7 (paperback)

Library of Congress Control Number: 2021950732

Contributors: University of Georgia Racial Trauma Task Force Members: Violeta J. Rodriguez, Dominique La Barrie, Kara West, Kelly Rea, Lauren Quast, Shannon McNally, Olutosin Adesogan, Erin Jones, and the EMPOWER Lab staff: Jeffrey Wes Unruh, Liana Giglio, and Yang Yu.

How did we make the C.A.R.E. Package?

1. **Assessment:** Who is the target population and what are their risk and protective factors? (Black youth, racial trauma, racial socialization)

2. **Decision:** What evidence-based programs (EBP) exist, and does it need to be adopted or adapted? (TF-CBT)

3. **Administration:** What in the original EBP needs adaptation, and how? (PRACTICE + racial socialization)

4. **Production:** First draft production and document adaptations? (postdoctoral research and clinical training)

5. **Topical Experts:** Who can help adapt the evidence-based program? (15 clinicians, 11 caregiver/youth pairs, 3 PhDs)

6. **Integration:** What will be included in the pilot adaptation? (This workbook!!)

7. **Training:** Who needs to be trained? (Trauma clinicians)

8. **Testing:** Was the adaptation successful? Did it enhance short- & long-term outcomes?

To make this C.A.R.E. Package, we worked with therapists, experts in Black youth development, and parents and teenagers who had experiences very similar to the ones we will discuss! The best part: there's science behind it all! We used the ADAPT-ITT Model to combine existing evidence-based strategies that we know work!

Who is this C.A.R.E. Package for?

Black Teenagers

Parents & Families

Friends & Community

Psychologists

Psychiatrists

School Counselors

Social Workers

I'm your C.A.R.E. Package Companion, and I'll be following along with you! Look for me as you go through the C.A.R.E. Package to help you explore your identity and answer questions you may have along the way!

Acknowledgements

Dr. Metzger would like to thank for their ongoing support, encouragement, and expertise:

- Yale University School of Public Health
    - Center for Interdisciplinary Research on AIDS
    - Research Education Institute for Diverse Scholars
- Dee Norton Child Advocacy Center
- The Cottage Sexual Assault Center and Children's Advocacy Center
- The Georgia Center for Child Advocacy
- Medical University of South Carolina
    - National Crime Victims Research and Treatment Center
- University of Georgia
    - The EMPOWER Lab
    - Racial Trauma Task Force
- Elmodern Graphic Designs

Contents

- What Types of Stressors do Children and Adolescents Experience?
- What Problems are Associated with Trauma Exposure?
- What are Social and Academic Consequences of Trauma?
- How Does Trauma Impact our Thoughts, Feelings, and Behaviors?
- What is Post Traumatic Stress Disorder?
- What is Racial Stress and Trauma?
- What is the Rain of Racism?
- What are the Four Levels of Racism?
- What are Microaggressions?
- What are Microassaults?
- What are Microinsults?
- What are Microinvalidations?
- How are Racial Stressors Traumatic?
- What are Common Reactions to Microaggressions?
- What are Fight, Flight, Freeze Responses to Racial Stressors?
- What are the Similarities Between PTSD and Racial Trauma?
- What is Racial Trauma?
- How Does Trauma Impact Black Youth?

Contents Continued

- What is Racial Socialization?
- What Are the Types of Racial Socialization Messages?
- How is Racial Socialization Communicated?
- How does Racial Identity Develop?
- How Does Racial Socialization Impact our Identity?
- What are the Benefits of Racial Socialization?
- How does Racial Socialization Impact Cognitive-Behavioral? Responses to Interpersonal and Racial Trauma?
- Skills for Healing from Racial Stress and Trauma
- Relaxation
- Progressive Muscle Relaxation
- PMR Practice
- Emotion Regulation
- Cognitive Restructuring
- How can Racial Socialization help in response to everyday stress?
- How can Racial Socialization help in response to racial stressors at school?
- How can Racial Socialization help in response to racial stressors in the community?
- Risk Reduction
- Congratulations from Dr. Metzger
- Resources
- C.A.R.E. Package Supplements

What Types of Stressors Do Children and Adolescents Experience?

Childhood trauma is the experience of an event that is emotionally painful or stressful, which can result in lasting mental and physical effects.

Each Year:
- 58% of youth experience or witness at least one trauma
- 15% of youth experience 6+ traumas

Types of Stressors Include:

- Sexual Abuse, Assault, or Exploitation
- Victim/Witness of Violence/Abuse
- Emotional Abuse
- Traumatic Grief

- Neglect, Failure to Protect, Endangering a Child
- Accidents & Disasters
- Medical Trauma
- War/Terrorism and Refugee

What are Social and Academic Consequences of Trauma?

Social Consequences

- Change in family relationships
  - Sexual abuse may change relationships with siblings/parents
- Change in peer relationships
  - Social withdrawal
  - Deviant peer groups

Academic Consequences

- Hopelessness impacts progress towards future goals
- Trauma reminders occur at school
  - Impaired concentration, increased vigilance & poor learning
- Somatic complaints (head & stomach aches) lead to missed school, poor grades, & dropout

How Does Trauma Impact Our Thoughts, Feelings, and Behaviors?

Inaccurate Thoughts

- "If you love someone, you show it physically or sexually."
- "Having a baby will show love."

Harmful Feelings

- Problems with emotion regulation
- Impacts self-esteem, self-worth, confidence, sense of identity

Risky Behaviors

- Behavioral modeling
- Avoidant and maladaptive coping
- Riskier sex
  - More partners
  - Unprotected sex
- Substance misuse

What is Post Traumatic Stress Disorder?

- Most youth heal from traumatic experiences with the help of their families, friends, and communities.
- Some who don't (up to 15% of girls, and 6% of boys) may develop Post Traumatic Stress Disorder (PTSD).

Stressor	• Exposed or Threatened
	   ◦ Death or Serious Injury
	   ◦ Sexual Violence

Intrusion	• Recurrent Distressing Memories • Dreams & Flashbacks • Physiological Reactivity or Distress After Exposure to Trauma Reminders

Avoidance	• Persistent, Effortful Avoidance of:
	   ◦ Thoughts and/or Feelings
	   ◦ External Reminders

Negative Changes in Thoughts & Mood	• Amnesia • Reduced Interest • Negative Beliefs • Detachment • Distorted Blame • Loss of Pleasure or Constrained Affect • Trauma Related Emotions
Arousal & Reactivity	• Irritability/Aggression • Exaggerated Startle • Self-Destructive Behavior • Concentration/Sleep Problems • Hypervigilance

What is Racial Stress and Trauma?

Dangerous or frightening race-based experiences that "overwhelm one's coping capacity and impacts quality of life and/or cause fear, helplessness, & horror…"

- Recent data on Black adults and **youth as young as 8** suggest
  - An average of **5 daily experiences** with racial stressors
  - Up to 90% report experiencing racial stressors **each week**
- Racial stressors can range in impact from stressful to potentially traumatic. Racial stressors can include:
  - An individual/direct experience
  - A witnessed/vicarious encounter
  - Ongoing collective experiences

Racial stressors are common, and when you experience them, it's important to know that you are not alone or wrong in your perceptions and reactions. What is an example of something that you have experienced or witnessed recently that was based on the color of your skin and was upsetting or stressful? This could be something like being followed around a store or seeing someone getting bullied online about their hair texture.

The EMPOWER Lab
ENGAGING MINORITIES IN PREVENTION OUTREACH WELLNESS EDUCATION & RESEARCH

What is the Rain of Racism?

Can be direct (discrimination in your daily life)

Can be indirect (viewing police brutality in the media)

Can take many forms
- Microaggressions
- Individual racism
- Institutional racism
- Environmental racism
- Systemic racism
- Vicarious racism
- Historical/Collective racism

Racism takes a negative toll over time

Parents, communities, and Trauma Clinicians can help youth deal with racial stressors as they form their identities

Like the rain, racism can erode and weather us over time. It can fall on you directly through daily interactions, or it can seep through a hole in the roof through faulty structures and systems. Who in your life is your umbrella? Where can you go for shelter from racism?

The EMPOWER Lab
ENGAGING MINORITIES IN PREVENTION OUTREACH WELLNESS EDUCATION & RESEARCH

What are the Four Levels of Racism?

Internalized racism
- private beliefs and biases about race that lie within individuals
- can take many different forms including prejudice towards others; negative beliefs about oneself; or internalized privilege

Interpersonal racism
- personally mediated, occurs between individuals
- bias that occurs with others wherein personal racial beliefs affect public interactions

Institutional racism
- occurs within institutions and systems of power
- unfair policies and discriminatory practices of institutions (schools, workplaces, etc.) that routinely produce racially inequitable outcomes for POC

Structural racism
- racial bias among institutions and across society
- compounding effects of societal factors, including the history, culture, ideology and interactions of institutions and policies that systematically privilege white people and disadvantage POC

Racism can take many forms. It is important to recognize how racism can manifest itself so that we can resist and fight back against the values, interactions, policies, and laws that are harmful and unfair. What are some examples of racism that you can identify at each of the four levels?

What are Microaggressions?

- Verbal, behavioral, or environmental slights
- Often automatic and unintentional
- Occur in brief instances on a daily basis
- Communicate hostile, derogatory, negative viewpoints
- Targets stigmatized or culturally marginalized groups

Types of microaggressions include:
- Microassaults
- Microinsults
- Microinvalidations

What are Microassaults?

- Less common, "Old-fashioned racism"
- Deliberate, conscious, and explicit
- Intention is to hurt, oppress, or discriminate
- E.g., "Jokingly" telling racist joke

What types of microassaults have you experienced or witnessed?

What are Microinsults?

"You speak so well for a Black person."

- Convey insensitivity, are rude, or demean an individual's identity or heritage
- E.g., "Where are you from?"

What types of microinsults have you experienced or witnessed?

What are Microinvalidations?

"Oh, I thought you were Chris. You two look the exact same."

- Exclude, negate, or ignore an individual's identity, thoughts or feelings
- E.g., Not acknowledging Black students' contribution, dismissing input from Black colleagues

"What types of microinvalidations have you experienced or witnessed?"

The EMPOWER Lab
ENGAGING MINORITIES IN PREVENTION OUTREACH WELLNESS EDUCATION & RESEARCH

How are Racial Stressors Traumatic?

1. Racial stressors are traumatic because they violate an individual's personhood and leave the victim feeling disempowered

2. Subtle acts may be worse than overt acts if the recipient of a racial stressor is challenged, ridiculed, or dismissed by others

3. Racially stressful events, like interpersonal violence, are unpredictable, uncontrollable, and potentially traumatic

4. In addition to healing from interpersonal trauma, some Black youth may need help coping with and healing from racial stressors

Racial stressors affect survivors in ways that are similar to the effect that rape and domestic violence have on their victims

What are Common Reactions to Microaggressions?

Psychological Consequences

- Anxiety
- Depression
- Sleep Difficulties
- Diminished Confidence
- Helplessness
- Loss of Drive
- Diminished Cognition
- Intrusive Cognitions

Internal Dilemmas

- Did I interpret that correctly?
- Did she say what I think she said?
- What did they mean by that?
- Should I say something?
- Saying something may make it worse.
- They'll probably think I'm overreacting.
- I should have been more prepared to speak up

What are Fight, Flight, Freeze Responses to Racial Stressors?

Fight
- Angry outbursts
- Non-compliance

Flight
- Avoiding peers, coworkers, colleagues
- Not participating in group activities

Freeze
- Delayed reactions
- Inability to respond to racial stressors in the moment

How do you typically react to racial stressors? Are there some that make you want to fight? Run away? Do you ever get stuck and not know how to respond in the moment? It is important to know that all of these reactions are normal.

What are the Similarities Between PTSD and Racial Trauma?

Experiencing racial stress, such as microaggressions, can often lead to racial trauma. The process by which this happens is very similar to that of interpersonal stress, such as physical abuse, to Post-Traumatic-Stress Disorder (PTSD).

Physical Abuse

Often unpredictable, with the recipient not being able to prepare to defend themselves

Common symptoms include:
Sleep disturbances
Rumination
Increased Startle Response
Low Self-Esteem

Microaggressions

Occur at any time & in public/private spaces. Recipients often caught off guard in how to respond

Common Symptoms include:
Sleep disturbances
Hypervigilance
Increased Startle Response
Avoidance

Racial Trauma and PTSD are almost identical with many similarities. Symptoms may vary between individuals, but the outcomes can be long lasting and have a negative impact.

What are some things that can help you and your family with racial trauma?

What is Racial Trauma?

Stressor	• Exposed or threatened death, serious injury, or violence • Direct or vicarious exposure to (racial) stressor
Re-Experienchg (1)	• Recurrent distressing memories • Reporting stressors (e.g., discrimination) in higher numbers
Arousal & Reactivity (2)	• Irritability / Aggression • Exaggerated startle • Concentration and sleep problems
Negative Emotions (2)	• Reduced interest • Detachment • Loss of pleasure or constrained affect
Avoidance (1)	• Persistent, effortful avoidance of: 　○ Thoughts and/or feelings 　○ External reminders

Racial trauma shares many mechanisms and health outcomes with PTSD. The connection between racial trauma and PTSD calls attention to the negative physical and mental health effects of racial trauma. Have you experienced these signs of racial trauma? What are some other potential symptoms?

How does Trauma Impact Black Youth?

MORE LIKELY:
- to experience trauma
- to experience racism and discrimination
- to suffer from mental health and behavioral consequences

MORE LIKELY:
- to use culturally specific protective processes within their families and communities

LESS LIKELY:
- to initiate trauma treatment
- to complete trauma treatment
- to report positive outcomes
- to sustain positive outcomes over time

How do you and your family heal? Black youth could benefit from using protective processes common to their family and community to help heal from stressors!

What is Racial Socialization?

Racial socialization is a series of conversations and interactions between Black caregivers and youth.

When adults pass on the values and practices of their ethnic group, they are participating in racial socialization!

When caregivers help youth prepare for and heal from negative racial encounters, they are delivering racial socialization messages!

If you are a Black youth or parent and you are having these conversations or participating in cultural activities with your family, you are engaging in racial socialization!

Most Black families are already doing this! There are tons of fun things that you can do and talk about with your family and friends to make coping with racial stressors relevant and beneficial to your family, community, and even society!

What are the Types of Racial Socialization Messages?

Racial pride messages: Teach children about Black heritage, history, and culture to promote group unity and combat negative experiences.

Racial barrier messages: Focus on preparing for, coping with, and healing from experiences with discrimination and racism.

Racial equality messages: Teach children that all races are equal and should live together peacefully.

Spirituality/Religious messages: Teach about religion and/or spirituality to promote strength, resilience, and empowerment.

Racial achievement messages: Focus on academic and individual achievement and the need for Blacks in America to work twice as hard as other groups to be rewarded the same.

Appreciation of extended family involvement messages: Emphasize the importance of others in child rearing and family management.

What kinds of conversations like these are you having now?

How is Racial Socialization Communicated?

How a family engages in racial socialization is based on the needs and desires of each family.

Families can transmit these messages *verbally*. For example, by discussing beliefs and values and helping youth problem solve.

Caregivers can *model behaviors* by demonstrating ways to respond to discrimination or by showing pride in their history and Black culture in day-to-day activities.
Exposure occurs when parents provide positive learning experiences like taking their children to historical museums.

Caregivers can *pay attention* to youths' interests and behaviors and engage in racial socialization by doing things like supporting youth in community activism and politics.

What new ways could you participate in racial socialization as a family?

How does Racial Identity Develop?

PRE-ENCOUNTER — Holds values of the dominant white culture; largely unaware of race or discrimination.

ENCOUNTER — A racist experience makes one realize they belong to a group that is discriminated against.

IMMERSION/EMERSION — Surrounded by people and symbols of Blackness and avoidance of whiteness.

INTERNALIZATION — Secure in one's Blackness; pro-Black attitudes become more expansive, open, and less defensive.

INTERNALIZATION-COMMITMENT — Has a plan of action with commitment to concerns of the Black community.

> Black identity develops through a process that varies from person to person. If you had to guess, where would you say you are in your racial identity development, and why?

How Does Racial Socialization Impact Our Identity?

 Racial socialization positively impacts our sense of self, others, and our future

Focusing on our African ancestry and celebrating historical and recent accomplishments of Blacks in America positively impacts our sense of self

 Understanding the difficulties of being Black in a white majority society impacts our sense of others and prepares youth for dealing with potentially negative racial encounters

Combined, having pride and being empowered promote resilience in youth and allow us to build and prepare for a better future

What are the Benefits of Racial Socialization?

- Racial socialization boosts self-esteem, racial identity, perseverance, and resilience and healthy coping.

- Racial socialization helps prevent negative emotions, behavior problems, and health difficulties after stressful life events.

- Healthy views of race help promote healthy decisions like abstaining from drug and alcohol use and avoiding risky sexual behaviors.

- Racial socialization encourages positive parent-child interactions, communication and support.

How else does racial socialization benefit you?

How does Racial Socialization Impact Cognitive-Behavioral Responses to Interpersonal and Racial Trauma?

Racial socialization is a cognitive behavioral strategy to address the needs of youth with PTSD, racial trauma and other difficulties related to stressful life experiences.

Before Racial Socialization	After Racial Socialization
Inaccurate/unhelpful thoughts	Realistic and helpful thoughts
Distressing feelings	Positive and calm feelings
Harmful behaviors	Healthy behaviors

Skills for Healing From Interpersonal and Racial Stress and Trauma!

Now, let's go over some skills:
- Relaxation
- Emotion Regulation
- Cognitive Restructuring
- Risk Reduction

Relaxation

- Relaxation is important for recharging, coping with stress, and healing from trauma. It is important to have ways to relax that can be used in different settings like at home or at school.
- A family's cultural background and values can affect how they respond to stress.
- A common racial socialization message is African Americans must work twice as hard to get half as much; and because of this, some Black families may place less importance on relaxation.
- We also recognize that with higher achievement must come greater attention specifically focused on relaxation and recharging.

Progressive Muscle Relaxation (PMR)

<u>PMR is a Technique used to reduce stress in your body by tensing and relaxing your muscle groups from head to toe</u>

- Elicit memories of a stressor that allows us to make the connection between emotions and feelings and to practice the skill
  - (e.g., heart beating fast, difficulty breathing, clenched jaws or fists, shaking legs)
  - **Relaxation** as **resistance** to **racism**

<u>Make examples culturally relevant</u>
- Start with breathing: Take air into your lungs and fill your body with peace
- Hands: "When life gives you lemons, make lemonade," Beyoncé album
- Shoulders: Carrying the weight of the world on your shoulders
- Arms: Stretch your arms towards the heavens
- Feet: After the rain comes sunshine, but there can still be mud

What is a stressful situation where you might use PMR to calm down?

PMR Practice (1/3)

What stressful situations do you or others in your community deal with?

Have you ever overheard someone making a racist comment? Have you or someone you know had a racist or scary encounter with the police? Have you noticed that you are treated differently because of the color of your skin? For example, someone watching you while you shop, people giving you dirty looks while hanging out with friends, or a group of people leaving you out of an activity because you're Black.

Think back to one of these times and remember how it made you feel. When we're upset or stressed, our bodies react in a certain way. Your heart might beat really fast, you might get sweaty, it may be hard to breathe, your body might feel shaky, it might feel like someone is sitting on your chest, you might clench your jaws or your fists…, your body may feel all sorts of ways. How does your body feel in these situations?

If you noticed that you have physical reactions in your body, this is why we sometimes call "emotions" our feelings-- because we can "feel" it when we're stressed or upset. This is an exercise that will help you relax in these types of stressful situations, called "Progressive Muscle Relaxation", or PMR. We relax our bodies because it let's us better handle our feelings, or emotions.

To do this, you can practice tightening your muscles and then relaxing them. This is a good way to relax because you can use it at home, in the car, at work, anywhere really! So, let's practice going through different muscle groups, one by one, to relax them.

PMR Practice (2/3)

To get started, you should get comfortable sitting in a chair, or lying down. Close your eyes and relax. Take nice, deep breaths in… and let it out slowly. Take nice, easy breaths… not too fast, or too slow… whatever is comfortable for you… notice that your body is starting to feel relaxed and calm… when you breathe out, feel your body become heavy and relaxed…

We know the saying that when life gives you lemons, you make lemonade. How do you make lemonade? By squeezing lemons, of course. Pretend you have two lemons in your hands, and you want to make lemonade. Take your hands and make tight fists, like you are going to squeeze the juice out of the lemons. Feel the tightness in your hand and arm as you squeeze. Now drop the lemon and relax. Let's try it one more time… Okay, now drop the lemon. Notice how your muscles feel when they are relaxed.

Continue to breathe but think about your arms. Tense your arms...like

you're showing off your muscles. Keep flexing as hard as you can….that's good...now relax your arms. Let's do that again… tense your arms super tight. Hold that tension. Now, let your arms fall back down and notice that they feel heavy and relaxed. Let them hang loosely on your lap.

Now think about your shoulders and your neck. Tense your shoulders by pulling your shoulder blades together and raising your shoulders up toward your ears. Tense the muscles in your shoulders. Hold it… now drop your shoulders and relax. One more time. Tense the muscles in your shoulders by pulling your shoulder blades together. Hold it… now drop your shoulders and relax. Notice that your arms and shoulders feel heavy and loose.

Breathe and relax, from your head down to your shoulders and arms

PMR Practice (3/3)

Do you ever notice that when you're stressed, you grind your teeth or clench your jaws? We hold tension in our mouths too. Tense your lower face and jaw by clenching your teeth and pulling the corners of your mouth backwards in an exaggerated grin, tensing the muscles in your lower face and jaw. It might feel silly, but go ahead and squeeze and tense your jaws like you're growling. Hold that tension. Now relax. Take a deep breath and feel the tension leave your face.

Tense your chest and stomach by taking in a deep breath and holding it, while making your stomach firm. Tense the muscle of your chest and stomach. Hold it. Now relax your stomach and take a deep breath in… and out. Let's take one more big breath in and hold it. Keep your chest and stomach firm. Breath out and feel your stomach and chest relax. Exhale.

Notice how good it feels to have relaxed muscles… now think about your legs and feet. Pretend that it just rained and there's a big mud puddle. Press your feet into the floor like you're sticking your bare feet in the warm, wet mud. Stick your toes deep in the mud… as far as they can go… good, now relax your toes. Take a few breaths. Stick your toes in the mud again...deeper into the mud, feeling it squish around your toes...now relax.

Notice how relaxed your body feels after tightening and relaxing your muscles. Continue to let all your muscle relax and focus on your breathing.

Now that you know how PMR works, when are times you could use it? What about when people treat you unfairly because of your race?

Emotion Regulation

The purpose of emotion regulation is to help recognize and communicate feelings you have about experiences with interpersonal and racial stressors.

Once you are able to identify and communicate your feelings, you can begin to tolerate distressing emotions and then to change the thoughts that you have about them that are inaccurate or harmful.

What recent experiences have you had with racial discrimination, and how did they make you feel?

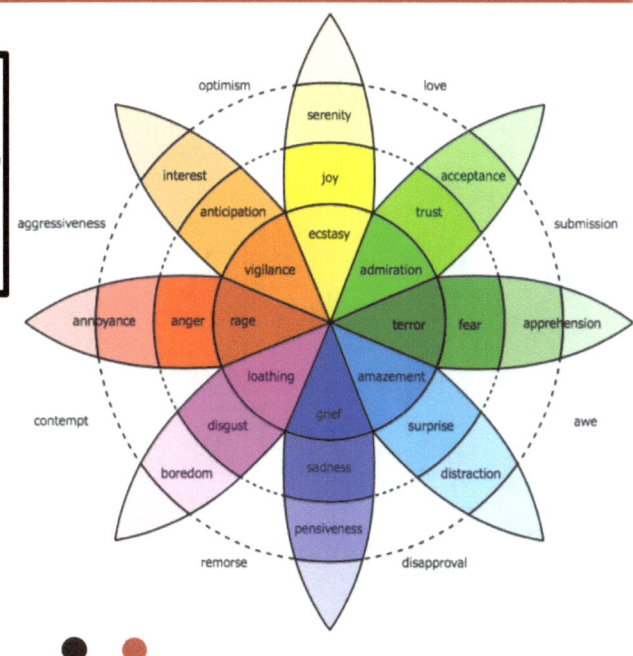

Cognitive Restructuring

Thoughts → Behaviors ↔ Feelings → Thoughts

The goal of cognitive coping is to learn the connection between our thoughts, feelings, and behaviors.

Cognitive coping allows you to evaluate the ways stressors you experienced may have impacted views that you have about yourself, the world, your family, and your future

There are many things that we can work on together to improve your cognitive coping abilities, including:

learning what to do in stressful experiences e.g., when pulled over by police, when followed by an employee, in situations with your peers involving sex, and drug use, and

learning how to regulate your thoughts and emotions after a negative racial encounter.

What was a recent stressful experience when you had a distressing thought or a negative emotion? What was the scenario? What did you think? How did it make you feel? What did you do?

How can Racial Socialization Help in Response to Everyday Stress?

Triggering Event: You walk into class and everyone starts laughing

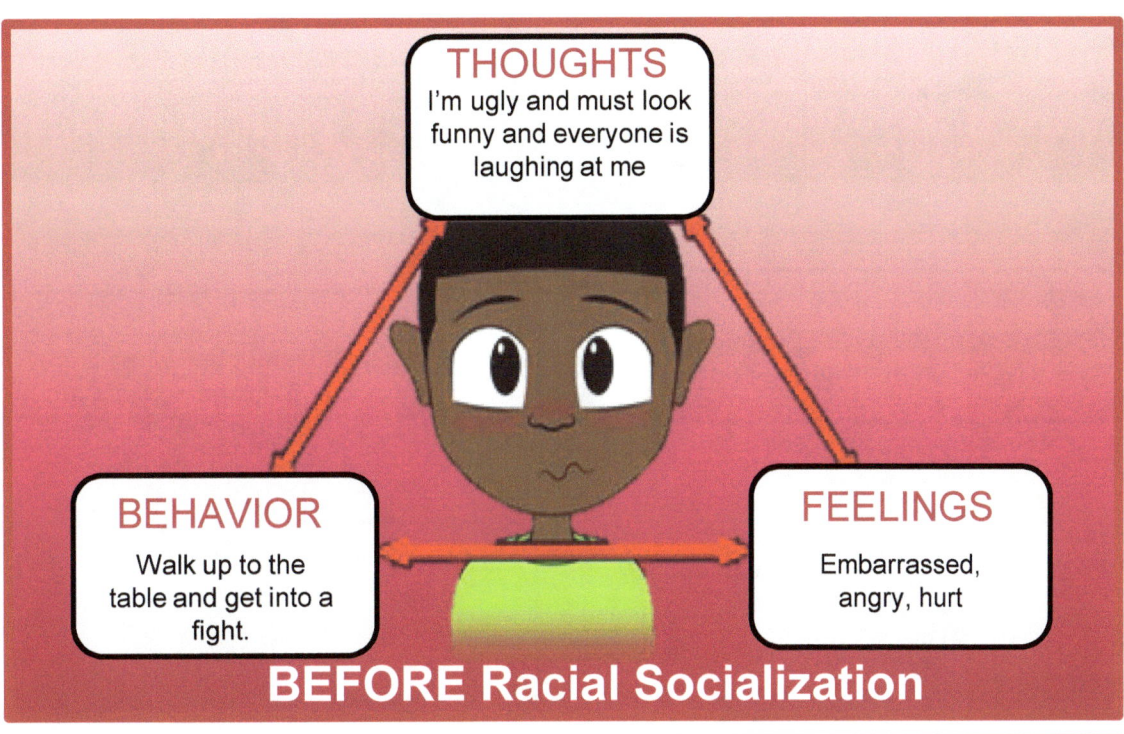

BEFORE Racial Socialization

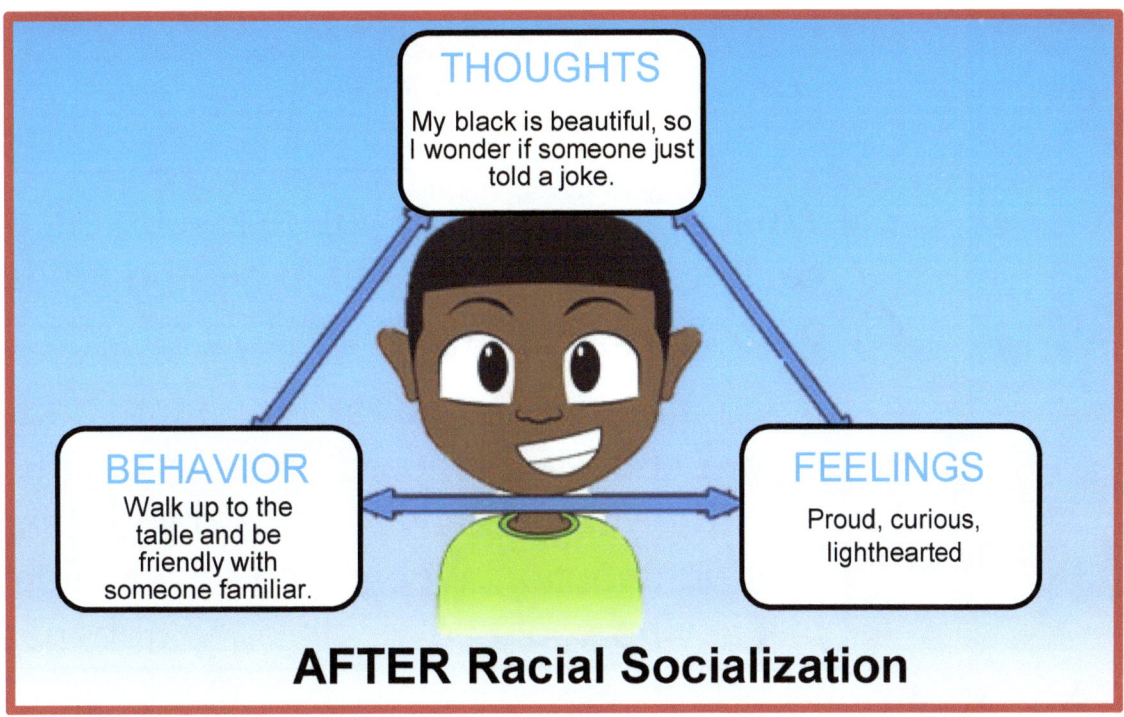

AFTER Racial Socialization

How can Racial Socialization Help in Response to Racial Stressors at School?

Triggering Event: You finish a group project and your teacher acknowledges everyone on your team but you

BEFORE Racial Socialization

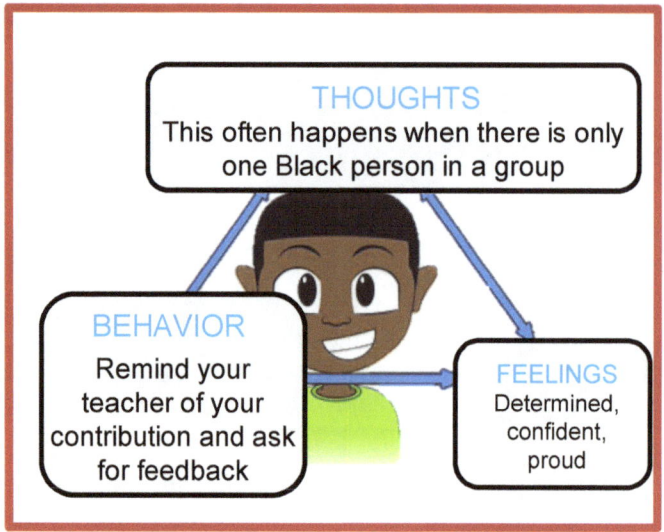

AFTER Racial Socialization

What questions could you ask yourself, or what could you say to yourself to get the grade and acknowledgement you deserve for your work?

If you already tried speaking up for yourself before and were ignored or disciplined unfairly, now that you're ready to remind your teacher of your contribution, who in your class might you talk to who could advocate on your behalf?

How Can Racial Socialization Help in Response to Racial Stressors in the community?

Triggering Event:
The driver of your car gets pulled over by the police

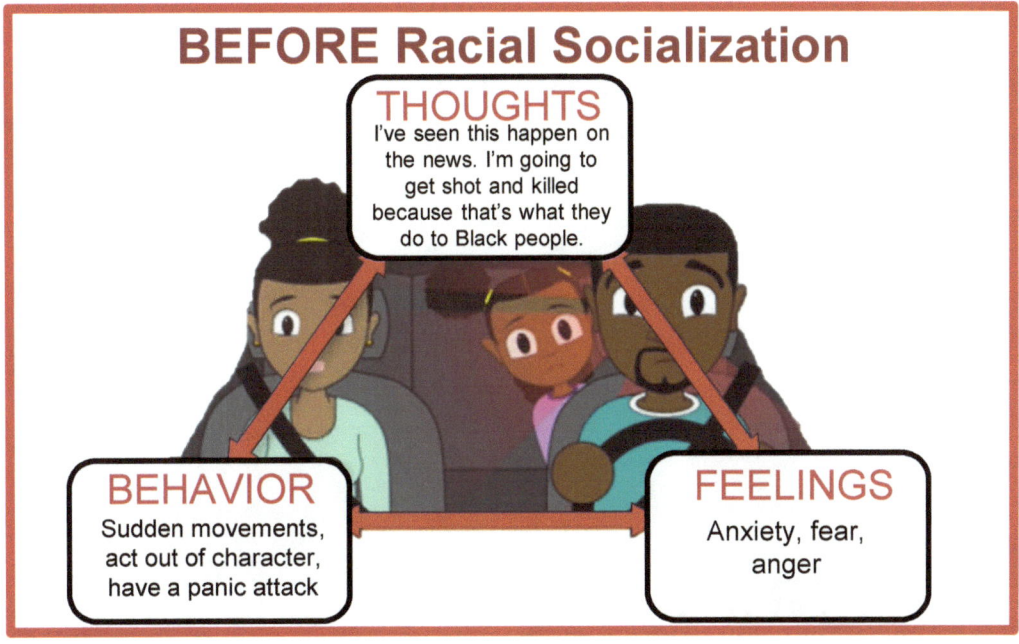

BEFORE Racial Socialization

THOUGHTS
I've seen this happen on the news. I'm going to get shot and killed because that's what they do to Black people.

BEHAVIOR
Sudden movements, act out of character, have a panic attack

FEELINGS
Anxiety, fear, anger

AFTER Racial Socialization

THOUGHTS
There is heightened racial tension, but I am prepared and know how to respond

BEHAVIOR
Hands at 10 and 2, respond with yes/no officer, use PMR

FEELINGS
Controlled, calm

What would you say to yourself, or what questions would you ask yourself in this situation to get from "Before" to "After"?

The EMPOWER Lab
Engaging Minorities in Prevention Outreach Wellness Education & Research

CONGRATULATIONS!

You took charge of Cultivating Awareness & Resilience through Empowerment and completed the Racial Healing C.A.R.E. Package! What are some things you can do to celebrate with your family?

1. _____
2. _____
3. _____
4. _____

RESOURCES

Trauma Focused Cognitive Behavioral Therapy Training
Medical University of South Carolina
https://tfcbt2.musc.edu

Anxiety Canada
www.anxietybc.com

The National Child Traumatic Stress Network
www.NCTSN.org

American Academy of
Child & Adolescent Psychiatry
www.aacap.org

The National Domestic Violence Hotline
www.thehotline.org

Isha W. Metzger, PhD
Isha.Metzger@uga.edu
www.DrIshaMetzger.com
www.instagram.com/theempowerlab

Resources: Being an Ally

- Racism and White Fragility: Combating Racism and Teaching Race Consciousness by Barry Foster
- How to Be An Antiracist by Ibram X. Kendi
- Between the World and Me by Ta-Nehisi Coates
- So You want to Talk About Race by Ijeoma Oluo
- We need co-conspirators, not Allies, The Guardian

- 10 steps to Nonoptical Allyship
- The myth of Colorblindness. Identity, Education, and Power
- Maintaining Professionalism In The Age of Black Death Is….A Lot
- Surviving the coronavirus while black
- A Parent of Color's Guide to Talking About Race
- A White Parent's Guide to Talking About Race
- Police reform since George Floyd's protests began
- COVID19 Resource Guide

- 13th
- When They See Us
- Just Mercy
- Selma
- If Beale Street Could Talk
- Hidden Figures

- "White Homework" by Tori Williams Douglass
- "1619", The New York Times
- "Hella Black Podcast" by Delency Parham and Blake Simons
- Bowtie Conversations "Talking to Children about Race"
- 'White Rage' and the pattern of punishing Blacks by Carol Anderson
- Opinion Science Podcast: Systemic Racism with Dr. Phia Salter
- Leading Equity Podcast: "I don't see color" with Dr. Rosa Perez-Isiah

Here are some things that you can watch, read, and listen to for info on being an ally.

Resources: Healing from Racial Stressors

- The Unapologetic Guide to Black Mental Health: Navigate an Unequal System, Learn Tools for Emotional Wellness, and Get the Help You Deserve - Rheeda Walker, PhD

- A Burst of Light: And Other Essays - Audre Lorde
- https://www.abpsi.org/pdf/FamilyCommunitySelfCareToolKit.pdf

- Black is King- A Film by Beyonce
- 40 Mins | Yoga Flow for Black Lives Matter | Self Care so you can Care for others
  https://www.youtube.com/watch?v=iK3iPlvY6g0
- I am not your Negro- Streaming on Netflix
- Coping Resources for Black Individuals and Families
  https://www.utoledo.edu/studentaffairs/counseling/diversity/copingresourcesblackindividuals.html

- "Hella Black Podcast" by Delency Parham and Blake Simons
- StreetWize Instrumentals
  https://www.youtube.com/playlist?list=PLxpwy7_IgqWRO6V_BJ79kAfoeBhrOZjBF
- "Therapy for Black Girls Podcast"- Dr. Joy Harden Bradford

Here are some things that you can watch, read, and listen to for info on healing from racial stressors.

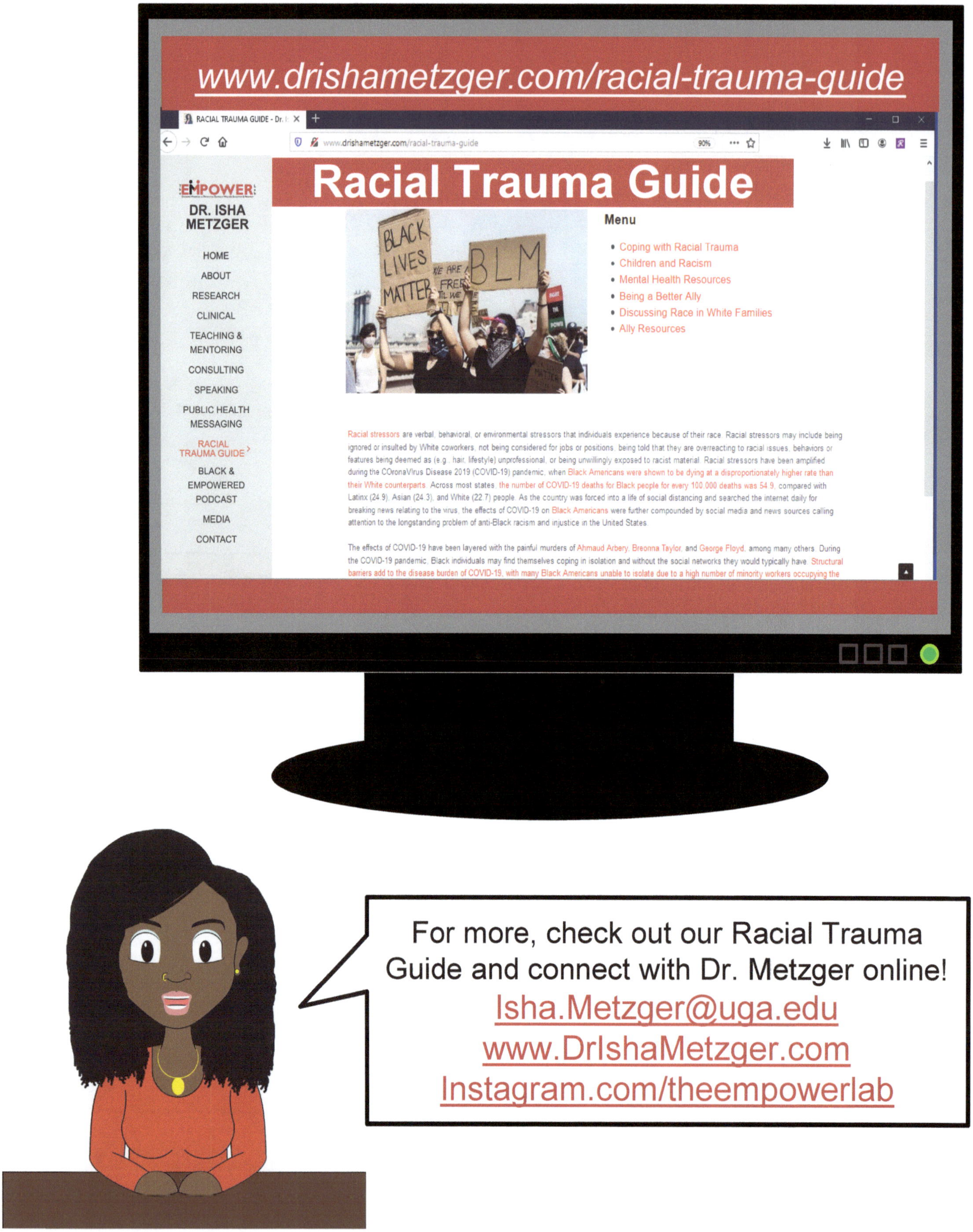

AUTHOR BIO
Dr. Isha Metzger

Dr. Isha Metzger is a first generation American from Atlanta, Georgia by way of Sierra Leone, West Africa. She is a Licensed Clinical Psychologist with a PhD in Clinical-Community Psychology from the University of South Carolina, Owner of Cultural Concepts Consulting, LLC, and Director of The EMPOWER Lab.

The overarching goal of Dr. Metzger's career is to take a strengths-based, anti-deficit approach to reaching youth of color. Dr. Metzger stands against anti-Black racism and oppression through "**E**ngaging **M**inorities in **P**revention, **O**utreach, **W**ellness, **E**ducation, & **R**esearch" using community-based participatory methods and advocacy. Both personally and professionally as an Assistant Professor of Psychology, Dr. Metzger is heavily invested in mentoring and training the next generation of community-based prevention scientists.

Though Dr. Metzger has authored and co-authored 39 manuscripts in peer-reviewed journals on topics concerning Black youth development, racial discrimination, racial socialization, and Black family processes, this is Dr. Metzger's first book.

THE C.A.R.E. PACKAGE
FOR RACIAL HEALING

SUPPLEMENTAL RESOURCES

Isha W. Metzger, PhD

Supplements

The following pages are activities, questions, and examples that you can use to supplement what you read in the C.A.R.E. Package!

- ❑ Prevent Trauma from becoming PTSD
- ❑ Racism in America is like the Rain
- ❑ The Four Levels of Racism
- ❑ Responding to Microaggressions
- ❑ Restructuring Relaxation
- ❑ 5 Ways to Cope in the Moment
- ❑ End Negative Self-Talk

PREVENT TRAUMA FROM BECOMING PTSD

Continuous **contact** with and **support** from important people in your life

Disclosing the trauma to loved ones

Identifying as a **survivor** as opposed to a victim

Use of **positive emotion** and **laughter**

Finding positive meaning in the trauma

Helping others in their healing process

Holding the **belief that you can manage your feelings** and **cope**

Reference: "How to Prevent Trauma from Becoming PTSD." ADAA.Org/, https://adaa.org/learn-from-us/from-the-experts/blog-posts/consumer/how-prevent-trauma-becoming-ptsd. Accessed 31 May. 2021.

RACISM IN AMERICA IS LIKE THE RAIN; IT CAN WEATHER EVEN THE TOUGHEST OF US.

You can **protect yourself** from **racism** just as you **protect yourself** from the **rain**!

[Learn more]

Your rainy day essentials:

- Your rainboots
- Your raincoat
- Shelter from the rain
- An umbrella
- Traveling to a dry area
- Fixing leaks

- Supportive friends and family
- A mental health professional
- Community centers
- Your mother
- Shopping at Black-owned businesses
- Being involved in your child's schooling

Source: https://earthbound.report/2020/12/09/the-four-levels-of-racism/

PERSONAL RACISM
a.k.a. internalized racism

- collection of prejudices and beliefs that every human being has, whether they are aware of it or not
- includes the feelings of superiority or inferiority

The media centers whiteness, favors lighter-skinned Black actors, and often portrays Black characters in a negative light

How have you noticed personal/internalized racism impact you and your loved ones?

Source: https://earthbound.report/2020/12/09/the-four-levels-of-racism/

INTERPERSONAL RACISM
the words and deeds of racist individuals

- bias
- bigotry
- deliberate discrimination

These could be blatantly racist remarks or more ambiguous microaggressions

You should go back to Africa!

So, where are you really from?

How have you noticed interpersonal racism impact you and your loved ones?

Source: https://earthbound.report/2020/12/09/the-four-levels-of-racism/

INSTITUTIONAL RACISM
racial inequality is embedded within institutions

- inequality can become ingrained in systems such as the police, schools, and healthcare
- includes policies or practices that treat people differently, even if it's entirely unintentional

Practices such as redlining, zoning, and the inequitable distribution of resources and discipline practices in school systems contribute to poor academic, behavioral, and physical and mental health outcomes, like school dropout, substance misuse, asthma, depression, school dropout, diabetes, and heart ailments

How have you noticed institutional racism impact you and your loved ones?

Source: https://earthbound.report/2020/12/09/the-four-levels-of-racism/

STRUCTURAL RACISM
a.k.a. systemic racism

- deeply embedded and multi-generational, patterns of exclusion that echo through society and reinforce disadvantage

The media and news often portrays Black men as dangerous criminals, intentionally characterizing them as menacing and deviant, which impacts policing, sentences, fines, and other legal penalties

How have you noticed structural/systemic racism impact you and your loved ones?

MICROASSAULTS:
How To Respond

ask a question:

> Why would you assume that I wouldn't be in an honors class?

> How did you get into this honors class? Haha

gently correct:

> That question is offensive to me. I do not need to prove myself to you.

state how it made you feel:

> I am just as qualified as you and our peers to be in this class; it is offensive to single me out and ask me that.

The EMPOWER Lab
ENGAGING MINORITIES IN PREVENTION OUTREACH WELLNESS EDUCATION & RESEARCH

MICROINSULTS:
How To Respond

Wow, you're so articulant!

ask a question:
Why do you find that surprising?

gently correct:
Although I appreciate a compliment, it sounds as though you were expecting me to be especially inarticulant.

state how it made you feel:
That comment is offensive because it sounds as though you initially assumed that I would not be very articulate because I am Black.

MICROINVALIDATIONS:
How To Respond

Why would having Black friends exempt you from saying or doing racist things?

I understand your thinking, but it's important to me that I communicate that what you did/said was racist, regardless of the fact that you have Black friends.

No, I'm not racist -- I have Black friends!

It upsets me when you say that because it minimizes the fact that you did/said something racist; rather than communicating and apologizing, it sounds as though you are in denial and will say/do it again.

The EMPOWER Lab
ENGAGING MINORITIES IN PREVENTION OUTREACH WELLNESS EDUCATION & RESEARCH

The EMPOWER Lab

@theempowerlab

Being Black, you have to work twice as hard to get half as far as a white person. So, we work, but we also rest and take the time that it takes to recover so that we can continue the work and spread our light along the way.

#racialsocialization #thetalk #restructuringrelaxation

5 WAYS TO COPE
IN THE MOMENT

 Count backwards from 20

 Grounding (e.g., name 5 things you can see, feel, hear)

 Tell yourself that your thoughts are just thoughts

 Positive self-talk ("I can handle this")

 Imagine a positive scene

End Negative Self-Talk

INSTEAD OF THINKING...

✕ Others are dangerous. I can't trust those people.

TRY THINKING...

✓ Lots of people haven't hurt me. Some people care about me and protect me.

INSTEAD OF THINKING...

✕ It's my fault that they did this to me. I should have known better.

TRY THINKING...

✓ I didn't do anything to cause what happened to me.

The EMPOWER Lab
Engaging Minorities in Prevention Outreach Wellness Education & Research

www.ingramcontent.com/pod-product-compliance
Lightning Source LLC
Chambersburg PA
CBHW050753110526
44592CB00002B/51